This is a beautiful work which touches us all in personal ways. As friends and spiritual brother and sister, I have benefited many times over the years from Jo's guidance, support and healing touch which she refers to as soultouch. I have found only jewels here and have been deeply touched by this work. This book is pertinent to many people at this time. It is honest and brave and I love the wit and play on words and turn of phrases. I also love and appreciate the way Jo expresses her vulnerability and turns it into strength with honesty and love.

I believe you will find this book to be both inspiring and uplifting.

Joseph Williams
Author, Poet and Fire Keeper

jewels in the garbage

Jo Levkoff

jewels in the garbage

Printed in the United States of America

ISBN: 978-0-578-86848-6

Cover design by Silver Lining Literary Services, LLC

Dedicated to the Goddess

Moira Brigit
you ignite my Muse
my Beloved
always

you guide me
through the depths
heart soul and spirit

flash in the dark
illuminate the invisible

ineffable
unconditional
love and gratitude

Jo

forward

Jewels in the Garbage is a phrase I first heard Dawna Markova say. Says so much so quickly. Sift what's useful. Throw the rest away. She also said: "Embarrassment is a step before enlightenment." I love that one too. I've had so many wonderful experiences, teachers, and friends who've put up with my pigheadedness and big heart. Jean Houston, Lynn Hoffman, Peggy Rubin, Deepak Chopra are huge influences in my life. I'm so blessed to have spent moments on the path with everyone I've met. So much gratitude only hints at what I feel.

One of the jewels in the garbage in this pandemic is I've expanded and had to commit to almost daily meditation practice to keep me sane, balanced, and fearless. Now each day I write for 19 minutes. Then meditate. Then stretch. The pages that follow are those writings. My musings, somewhat stream of consciousness, slightly edited, sometimes. Raw me writing. Sift whatever's useful. Throw the rest away. Thank you, bless you for taking the time to sit with me and spirit.

19 june 2020

it's been so long
since I let you out
soul trapped in my unwillingness
to write
to right
the wrongs
and thus create more

selfish to put pen to blank page
and see whatever is revealed

why would the muse come
if I don't invite her
and make the time and space
to welcome
her into my life

20 june 20

care for the temple

breathe deep
and be aware
stop several times each day
breathe in a non-habitual way
be home and be peace
in this temple of the soul
breathe deep and sing gratitude to the trees
when beliefs behaviors and breathing
become habitual
being unwell begins

shake hard
especially when feeling anxious
slough off cellular memory
dislodge the sludge that no longer serves

be present
ground
only mother earth really knows
how to hold me
and take the stresses of the day away
when I lay still with her on her
sometimes stretch and roll
we massage and heal each other

when I withdraw my attention
from the violence tragedy and craziness

in the world right now
and focus on the stillness and peace
in my heart and soul
I remember to breathe deep

21 june 20

until now

if I am not my own spiritual ally
how can I be an ally with anyone else
I've known from a very young age
that writing helps me connect with me
with my soul. I'd stopped writing.
until now

22 june 20

"the silence in our hearts is our essence our true self"

Deepak day 21
creating peace from the inside out

today
sinking feeling
like a toilet flushing
whirlpool swirls down
even a piece of shit
is eventually
compost for new growth

23 june 20

forged

between anvil and hammer
pounded smashed
one blow after another
sparks fly
dull dangerous rough edges
smoothed sharpened
honed to perfection
rapier

cut through ego
once and for all

24 june 20

meditation
no thought
no feeling
no sensation
no ego
silence in the heart
a rare moment

sometimes my love
of thought feels more important
than being with my soul
no thing is more important

I watch thoughts come
feel the muscles in my face tense
until I consciously stop thinking
and relax
spiritual practice

home to me

spark of spirit
inhabits this temple
free to float
in infinity
and merge with
whatever experience
is necessary
for my spiritual growth

25 june 20

bug duty

we found Harris's Asian Beetle Killer
it decimates lady bugs centipedes and stink
bugs
just vacuum up
odorless stainless
used inside and out
safe for pets and the environment
how is this possible

Stop bugging me
all the little flying creepy crawlies of life
stop
distracting me
if I can't change my attitude
kill the buggers

maybe original sin is self judgment

26 june 2020

heart to heart

where is my heart
surely not in here
where it belongs
hiding somewhere
even I cannot find the delicate organ
trompled
eaten
consumed with grief
crushed every time
I remember how I’ve hurt you
memory fails
I don’t want to remember
you remind me every day
I run

if I forgive myself for despicable acts
why do I repeat the behavior

27 june 20

I cannot change what I'm not aware of
like
habits
how I deal with stress is unconscious
take breathing
if I hold in emotions for one reason or
another
I'll be holding my breath in some way
certainly not breathing as deeply
and not taking in as much chi and O2 as I
need
more inflammation
and dis ease

breathe deeply
with non-judgmental compassion
and forgive
self

awareness is the change

28 june 20

empty quiet still
in my heart
the sky outside
heavy grey shrouds
lush greens
so grateful
for this moment

I set the timer
so I needn't think about time
yet here I am
thinking about time

paradox everywhere
help me understand
the difference between
paradox and hypocrisy
saying something
doing something else
how can I trust me more

29 june 20

staring at this blank page
nothing else matters
except my commitment to the muse
show up
see what comes
trust whatever
is meant to be

30 June 20

writing postponed
to fell the myrtle
exhausted after
slug is today's totem

1 july 20

ode to a crepe myrtle

20 plus years ago
on another's recommendation
we planted a crepe myrtle
near the back deck
as she grew
she offered shade
and beautiful pink bouquets
later in the summer into fall
several years ago
she began to block
our view of the goddess
two not so distant hills
rolling into each other
breasts concealing Round Mountain
in the distance
mons of the goddess
yesterday
we offered gratitude
and tobacco and then cut
her to the ground
we burned what we could
and will use her slender arms
to help hold in the mountain
recycling and composting
her gifts

now the view is clear
I can see the goddess in all her glory

I feel a lightness and freedom
I can breathe a little deeper now
and something has
shifted inside
I see more clearly

this growing awareness
if I make a commitment
to spiritual practice
to honor this soul's journey
and I don't keep it
how can I possibly trust me
if I say I want to do something
and I don't do it
how can I possibly trust me
however I rationalize it
I'm betraying my soul

If I am not an ally on the path with me
how can I be an ally with you

which stone do I want to ripple in the pond

2 july 20

life is a lie
when I take out the 'f'

take out the fun
what the F

everything outside
the pandemic
mixed messages
chaos
fear
tempest on the ocean
waves violent
surge crash destroy
yet deep underneath
still silent peace
expanded awareness

we're all in this school of life
learning what
to come home
and re member
the miracle and blessing
being born human

what are the chances
think about how many bugs there are or trees
heck we could have been born
a snake or a turkey or even a cockroach

3 july 20

meditation on stuckness

doing the same thing over and over
getting the same result
habitual insanity
breeds
misery

awareness in the moment
creates choice
do I want to keep being stuck
do I want something different
my choice with awareness

practice non-habitual behaviors
drive new roads
take a breath instead of seething
growl without words
bathe in dawn's precious light
dance in the rain
experience a starry night

4 july 20

this Independence Day
Deepak's teaching is on resistance
how ironic
he's talking about resistance to change
to letting go of the past
getting present
embracing the realm of infinite possibility
and whatever comes
with an open heart and mind

as the pandemic rages
people with awareness
rage at the injustice
of treating any person
who is not a white male
differently
under the law
what happened to
treating others as I want to be treated

how did we as a nation so devolve
how did I so devolve
let me claim honor and release
my own hypocrisy

out of chaos
creativity
a new dawn
a new day

5 july 20

about fear stress and anxiety

fear comes with imminent threat
lion tiger or bear
when the threat leaves
the fear leaves

not so in these pandemic days
thinking about that
added to thinking about global warming
and thinking about nuclear stockpiles
and thinking violence on the streets
it makes sense to feel fear stress and anxiety

actually other than exercise our right to vote
when it's time
what purpose does thinking about that stuff
and feeling anxious about all that serve
except to keep us confused and powerless

so simple
stop thinking
be present
peace beauty and truth
are waiting within

be fearless
embrace whatever comes
as exactly what is needed
for soul to connect with spirit

6 july 20

In the vastness of the universe
we are but tiny specs of dust
infinitesimally miniscule and yet
look at the drama we create –
life and death
we separate part of ourselves
and forget we are one
that feeling of disconnect
not belonging
is what we do to ourselves

forgetting is the original sin

“missing the mark” is one of the meanings of
sin
what’s the mark
boundary
omen
sign

signs are everywhere
when I’m present and grateful
when I’m not
I miss the mark

forgetting what I see
in the mirror of life
is me
the beauty

the magic
the conflict
the stress
my responsibility
to embrace or resist
resist grows the sense of separateness
embrace grows the sense of belonging
resisting creates an inner war and outer violence
embracing creates inner peace and outer compassion

choose wisely

7 july 20

“I seek true fulfillment within”

today
I changed my practice
to notice differences
instead of stretching first
I meditate sitting
then stretch now write

more aware of physical sensation and
discomfort
my thinking almost ran amok
occasionally I witness and remember
the mantra and my breath

awareness of sensation leads to more
thinking for me

one of the thoughts was of Nana
an image of her so long ago with her new
charges
hearing Nana say my name
Joey Ellen
with her German accent
mien liebchen

she bathed me in unconditional love
there at my birth till I was 4
she encouraged and praised me for
being me exploring everything

she never said no

an Auschwitz survivor
her parents and fiancé killed there
she said I was the first being who brought
love back into her life

I saw her numbers and asked and asked
she never told her story to me
I don't know if she ever told it

years without contact
I learned
she'd had several bouts in rehab for drink
I found her again
in a nursing home with dementia
she did recognize me

remembering Nana
brought a smile in my heart
warmth radiating love

that place has always been there
sometimes I just need a little help
to remember
who I am

8 july 20

connecting with soul

only awareness
in the stillness of my heart
do I hear the silent whisper within
soul connecting with spirit

I thought because I know
everything I say and do
comes from soul
my life is blessed
and on some level that's true
on another a lie

if I don't believe this relationship
me with M(us)e
is more important than
everything and everyone else
if I don't commit to that practice
of taking time to be alone with Thee
and write reflections
then I betray me

then I betray the Beloved
then I betray you

don't take it personally

9 july 20

spiritual healing
can only happen within
when I uncover
essence without ego
of who I am

one with all

ego separates
soul connects

what choice
do I really have

10 july 20

pointed

who sharpens the point
of a javelin
and how
hammered on an anvil
ground on a stone
filed to pointed perfection
I am that blade
weary
yet ready
to fly
on the mark

who throws the spear
and to pierce what
my heart and soul
yours

I am
all of the parts
of the story
whole
holy

11 july 20

sleep won over writing
I ran out of time this morning
before work
so exhausted
weary
with the heat
the pandemic
the job
choices
body or soul
how do I exquisitely care
for all of me
so tonight
before sleep
I write
grateful
to be with You

12 july 20

playing with you

writing
while the coffee's hot
instead of stretching first
meditating
then writing

savoring a cuppa Joe
my dear Friend
I drink for you
for Krishna
for this blissful moment
where the infinite realm
of possibility
and we
are one

getting ready
for the drama of work
as a Lowe's cashier
in a town where 2/3's of the cars
in the parking lot
are from out of state
in a pandemic

the president finally wore a mask today
our 'leader' may think he's immune
and maybe his money will buy him the best
care if he needs it

the guidance he models
for folks who don't have his money
the rest of us
puts our lives
at greater risk of expiring
sooner than later

what a cosmic joke
choices

do I focus within
or without
my decision

13 july 20

playing again

as long as I commit
my time and attention
to be with you
fully present

and witness
without judgment
with compassion
and a little humor
when I am not
aware

I grow closer to you
immerse myself in you
you gift me
infuse every breath
oh the day

commit is the operative word
I watch in the silence
as noises rise
sensations
feelings
thoughts
distractions all

mantra
breathe

commit to being present
in the silence
of my heart and soul

close to you

14 july 20

when the unexpected arises
be flexible
even if that means
putting my commitment aside
temporarily

I'm coming back to you
soon
please wait for me
I hope not lifetimes
nor years
like in my recent past
not months or days
maybe minutes hours
maybe it's all now anyway

even if I miss taking time to be with you
one day
I shall double up on the next
if you'll have me
will you
will you be there for me
no matter what
even if I'm not there for me

sounds like the goddess to me
what luck
what a blessing

when I learn to be here for me
no matter what

even if I lie
even if I steal
even if I break an agreement
with you

I enter the realm of infinite possibility
where unconditional
compassion and love
abide always

what joy

15 july 20

fascinating
how a change in practice time
throws off my motivation
for meditation

the discipline
I need to come home
I so love to run
anything will do to distract

thank the goddess
I have the privilege
to be semi-retired
and spontaneous
to sit and write
any time of day

when my time with you
each day ends
I feel a strange fullness
oddly empty
overflowing
abundance
gratitude
for just a snippet
of peace joy and love

let it grow let it grow let it grow

16 july 20

19 minutes to write
that's all I give myself
when time feels limited
by outside commitments

precious moments
wasted
waiting for the computer
to kick in
and actually work

yet in this exquisite now
aware that everything is a mirror
the apple god controlling this device
and my process
must know better
knows I need to learn patience
and trust
in the process
everything happens
in exactly the moment
it needs to happen in

it is so easy
to get caught up
in the external drama
I feel sensation
then emotion
and think
I need to act

impulsively
and then
deal with
the consequences

eventually
with awareness
unskillful behavior
can lead to
healing

the key

17 july 20

what do I mean by awareness

the experience
of witnessing
without judgment
or attachment
watching clouds float

images stories feelings
come and go with the wind
urged and shaped by
Someone
or
Something
breathing

god
the goddess
mother nature
whatever energy creates
this magnificent life

stories
I create
with how I respond
to external events
like the story
of my life

aware

from the still silent
infinite
heart space

infinite
peace
bliss
beauty
delight
compassion

18 july 20

6 minutes of the 19
I give myself to write
stuck in limbo
word on page blocked
by an old computer
on its deathbed

do I waste time
feeling frustrated
scheming how to
get a new one
or save time
breathing deep
feeling gratitude
for this one precious moment

aware of choices

one is habit
the other new neural pathways

one creates more stress
the other more bliss

what choice

19 july 20

stretch
write
meditate
does the order influence
the written word

when I light the candle
and feel gratitude
for a whole hour
to be present
in body
mind
soul
and spirit

I smile big
heart melts
everything outside disappears
in this precious moment

so what's the difference
between soul and spirit

soul is a tiny wee toty bit
of spirit
spirit embodies all soul
in the infinite realm of possibilities

connected

belonging
we are one

when I forget
my connection
I start a war within
violent to myself
I do the same to others
till I own the reflection

20 july 20

meditate
write
stretch

being auditory
phrases
like images
float by

spiritual mutt

maybe body wisdom
with awareness
is wiser than mind
maybe post nasal drip
is body's way of telling me
I'm swallowing tears
there's a deep sadness
in there

once I let myself feel the depths
on a training retreat
during a meditation walk
around a New Hampshire lake
as I step with awareness
surrounded by exquisite beauty
I see a cigarette butt and a
crumbled beer can on the ground
and out of nowhere

this tsunami of tears
moved through
I sobbed for three hours

what have we done to this magnificent earth
what have we done to each other
how did we get so far from love

21 july 21

10 years since Buddie died
me mum
would've been 95 today
wherever you are
gratitude and blessings

not any sadness there
there was love
we were not the best of pals

sadness now
I gird myself from
lots of people are dying
because our government
and infrastructure was not prepared
focused on greed
hospitals are now at the tipping point

pandemic
epidemic
endemic
to a belief that profit and power for a few
is more important than the well being of the
many

in a just society
putting the well being of the people first
will create greater profit for all

what you gonna do
go on with love
whatever you do
I was writing
go on with life
and love got writ

spirit works in mysterious ways

lots of people are dying
we're killing each other
for money

go team

22 july 20

how can I prove
this soul stuff works

most of us are scared shitless
to go that deep
myself included

worth is inside
core of who we are
heart and soul
true self
love peace joy compassion delight

no one can take that away
they can try
even if I buy into their lie
worth is still in me
just guarded

withdrawn proposal
released the project with
peace and justice

head stuff
interferes with heart and soul

23 july 20

writing now
meditating and stretching later
starting late in the day

don't feel like much of doing anything
slug totem kicking in
I want to be irresponsible
pull the covers over my head
sleep eat watch movies
not see anyone
not talk with anyone
be completely alone
in my own energy
which isn't very much now

I'm so distracted
get the heck out of dodge
run away

angry
hurt
I don't care anymore
whatever will ease being
I want that
tired of being in the bardo
tired of being your perp

mutually exclusive dreams
make for conflict and pain

24 july 20

steady rain
lightning
thunder
they're bowling upstairs
strike
me
lay me
wide open

nothing more to say

waiting

for word from you
to come through

while waiting

silence
welcomes me
unconditionally
enfolds me
holds me
is here for me
whenever I show up
no matter how many years
I've been away
she is here for me
in me

when I sit
in her embrace
when I come to her
wide open

no thought
no feeling
no sensation
no ego

connected to source
soul to spirit

the outer world
distraction
slowly
disappears

how to be of service
home alone
just us
with Freedom and Trust

25 july 20

writing
meditating
stretching

when I write first
I'm closer to the dream time
tho I've not remembered a dream
in decades
still...

that's the whole point
of meditation
isn't it
getting to that place
of peace stillness silence
our very center
begins to infuse
the rest of life

no more allies out there
letting go of that dream
bashed the last bit of ego armor
no where to run
no where to hide
no one in the world

trusting soul
being love

26 july 20

the thing about writing first
is the coffee is still hot
"let the soft animal of your body
love what it loves"
thank you Mary Oliver
and the goddess of ease and pleasure

is awareness
simply
witnessing
without judgment
whatever is

I have heard that
ego and soul
are mutually exclusive

ego is needed
to exist in the world outside
soul is needed
to be in the inner world

events on the outside
can be a portal to going within
with awareness

experience on the inside
can infuse events on the outside

the point of intersection
infinity symbol
lemniscate

all that is this little speck of dust
called
me

27 july 20

washer and dryer on
adding to the om of the universe
or is it
noise
distracting me
from presence
choices

feeling a moment
of despair
really really low
why bother being here
no meaning
in work out there

then searing anger
lightning thunder
why is this country
paying people to not work
and not paying the same amount
to the people risking their lives working

where are our fucking values

everything out there
points to
look within

what an amazing

opportunity
to
grow
soul
infinite
unconditional
love and compassion
within

stone splashes in a pond
ripples ripples ripples
reach the shore
then float back home

28 july 20

slow reader

45 minutes to get through
an 8 page single spaced
dharma talk by Joan Halifax
on rites of passage and honoring
personal and global grief and fear

grief is love that has nowhere to go
fear helps us learn about boundaries

slow learner

29 july 20

turning off notifications

I thought I'd turned off all the beeps and
whistles
of my iphone but no at 6am a bell rings
wake up
I mumble grumble
then gratitude for the day
and for someone reaching out

can't go back to sleep
sleep is a most precious commodity
sleep and meditation
especially these days

a wake up call comes
when least expected
spirit demands
a response
open to the unknown
or keep the door closed

ah choices

I prefer waking up on my own
without an alarm
spirit this morning
prefers otherwise

ding

I get up
not necessarily awake
write a brief note
and click send
at 7

how rude of me
too early
doing just what I grumbled about

if you haven't turned off
your notifications
I might have sent you
a wake up call

30 july 20

light a candle
and smile
what a thrill to be able to take this time
to be with You
oops
where are the matches
find another box
now light the candle
oops

right under the candle holder
matches
talk about not seeing
what's right in front of me

how else do I do that

is writing
more important
to my soul
than meditating

in writing
I'm more focused
on allowing presence
in the present

in meditating
my mind has

more of a tendency
to run amok
I watch
as I rush off
into this thought
or that feeling
and think it through
or feel the depth
then let it go

sometimes
my witness
sees thinking
and I take a breath
remember the mantra
and get present

only a moment later
on its own volition
the thought returns
because it needs my
undivided attention
and I need my
unconditional compassion
noticing how I habitually
get distracted in the silence

in the silence
connection with You

so grateful
for each precious moment

31 july 20

masked nation
no
make that world

we're all wearing masks anyway
what's the big deal

if there's a possibility
I could be a carrier without knowing
and my wearing a mask would protect you
from getting that virus
of course
I'd want to do that

if I didn't
I could be a murderer
maybe I am

so spirit is saying
it's time to look at
all the different masks
I wear
perhaps I wear
a different mask in different situations

who's behind the mask

soul

I learned to
cover up who I really am
how I feel
what I think
to avoid
other people's judgments

and then it's habit
I have to put my face on
make up
in the morning
showtime folks

make up what
what face is that
whose face

surely not mine
not heart and soul

own the mask

take it off
when safe
be
true to heart and soul

ps...on this day my computer's time machine
the external backup of the entire contents
herein all the past is gone and we need to
start a new backup how's that for a message
to be present

1 aug 20

distracted by ego
imagining a conversation
I might have
that may open
a new portal
actively asserting
what I want
not waiting
for spirit to bring
another opportunity
for right livelihood

spirit
grateful for all
you send my way

and I'm ready for a change
gratitude always for your
unconditional support

breathe
mantra
be present
notice

reflecting on
when I take off my mask(s)
who am I

if I am

believe speak and act
true to heart and soul
consistently
in every situation

then the only time
I'd wear a mask
is outside
if I am closer than 6 feet to you
or in a building with lots of people

if I'm a carrier of a deadly virus
and I don't know it because
I'm symptom free
and I give it to you
well that would be just awful

I'd want to protect you from that

so mask   on

2 aug 20

if I am unaware
I will act out
unskillful behavior

If I'm not paying attention
you could be next
friends family work
a complete stranger
might get dumped on

at home
I feel
enough love and safety
for me
to risk
all of me
if I break an agreement
you point that out
with ouch that hurts

I can see
some soul agreement
I'm breaking with myself

something I've been
unwilling to look at
in me
so I learn
at your expense

if I honor this soul agreement
me with me
then I will honor any other agreement I make

long pause
as I hear
as long as the agreement
includes a change clause

saved by the bell
that's all for today

3 aug 20

warming my heart
waiting for words to come
enjoying a cuppa Joe
resting on my heart
warming
melting
whatever gets me there
to that sweet merging
thoughts disappear
muscles relax
skin evaporates
no more me
one with everything
just in a taste of silence

so this coffee thing
this addiction
I get headaches
without the stuff
is guiding my spiritual practice
at the moment

soft animal of this body
wants to savor the moment
hot coffee better than cold
light a candle
then write
meditate
stretch

playing has yielded a plan
that any given moment
can change again
that's the nature of now
don't hold me
to what I've said or done
in the past
hold me now

completely brand new
now is

4 aug 20

eat my words
so quickly
plans change
Mo's not well
could be going through
old moldy papers
could be
covid 19
trouble breathing
really bad headache

it's after noon
sleeping now

service
seva
stand vigil
smudge

please goddess
let this be a reaction to mold
I cannot bear to think
I brought the virus

energy for deep healing
a shamanic journey
coming out
of the dark night
healthier than ever

5 aug 20

way better
our dear neighbor
made chicken noodle soup
from scratch
which I ate while
Moira slept 16 hours

then
thinking I need to do another treatment
of the mildew and mold
in the house
I proceed to mix vinegar and tea tree oil
in the kitchen
while Moira
is making her breakfast

her nose started running
blood pressure rising
she thinks I did it on purpose
to harm her

I was thinking about treating things
to help make the house more safe
not thinking in the moment
that smelling tea tree will
be an affront to her
sensibilities and healing

when is thinking I'm being thoughtful

thoughtless
when is thinking I'm being helpful
harmful
I suppose it's another type
of unilateral decision
on something that effects
both of us

what do I need to learn
here

is it simply habit
do what I want to do
is it something more dark
intentionally hurtful

I'm not willing to own that

ask before acting
I'm thinking about doing this now
you good with that

I thought I was doing so well
during this healing crisis
I asked how I could help
I guarded your sleep
I lit candles and smudged
for healing and
the best possible outcome
then a bit of hell breaks loose
I act unskillfully
again why

6 aug 20

cupboard with mildew
destroyed
prybar and chainsaw
decimated
the source of the headache
we think
the parts saved salved
in tea tree and vinegar
kill the mildew

wood burned in ceremonial fire
releasing all the mildewed moldy
beliefs and practices
that make us sick
claiming the magnificent
healing temple this body is
when relaxed and at peace

oh to be present

7 aug 20

distracted from practice
outside calls
things to do
yet
I know in every cell
of my being
there is
nothing more important
than being with the goddess
god
spirit
whatever we call our higher self
soul

the idea is
the more I practice
be with spirit
and taste the silence
feel love
peace
bliss
the greater the possibility
this infuses the rest of life

what do I mean by spiritual practice
write
meditate
stretch
be

awareness
exquisitely present
unconditional compassion and love
practice never ends
a lifetime commitment

that's a lot of work
no wonder I run

sometimes I just want
to be irresponsible
sloppy
unconscious

not for too long
but sometimes
I don't want to do anything
I want to watch the grass grow
sit with my feet in the creek
do nothing

I suppose
that's the whole point
of meditation

what else do I mean by spiritual practice

8 aug 20

after prayers
so grateful for this
soul's time with spirit

I set the timer
for 19 minutes
then wait for the computer
to wake up
and the software to kick in
so I can begin to write

how do I use the waiting time
the unknown time
bardo time
where details of the past
are simply erased

vague feelings
without words

and no clear sign
that the future
can be anything other
then repetition of the past

in that place
the waiting time

when I stop thinking
now is all there is
in the realm of infinite possibility

the feelings in now
gratitude
ease
peace
wide open heart
unconditional
bliss

9 aug 20

sitting on the shitter
I read something
in the news
independent.co.uk
all the same eh

news in the world
is pretty shitty

microcosm
macrocosism

mirror mirror

live backward
is evil

after reading the news
this morning
I had evil
thoughts
I thought about payback
and murder

I would never act on those thoughts
I own I have them

I have a fascination

with stories about serial killers
the holocaust
war

once upon a time
I worked with people
who described
surviving cult abuse
I was a therapist
the rapist

I have to look at the dark side within
hello Darth Vadar

embrace it with
unconditional compassion

anything less
I'll see in you

the notions of dark shadow black
become bad
for people that don't own
their inner darkness
violence to self
means hurting others
unconsciously
intentionally

choices

10 aug 20

everything is a lesson
in this present moment
this very now

I go to write
on my 8 year old
dinosaur of a computer
and she's having trouble getting it up
the software
again

there's a little spinning rainbow ball
that's saying
if you can speak computer
I'm working really hard
my wheels are spinning
trying to get this thing in gear

kind of like being stuck
in a thought feeling or habit
If I interfere in any way
judging
mocking
fixing
that little sphere
spins a lot more

it takes much longer to get unstuck

when I sip my coffee
smiling
grateful for this moment
to be still
and hold the space
let the feeling
run its course
and come to stillness

it changes all by itself

with awareness
in the present
miracles are everywhere

11 aug 20

forget the past
and trust

everything
that ever happened
a dream

fog fading into

this present moment
soul in body
breathing
grateful

trust intuition
and spirit
before any
idol or idea

even this

12 aug 20

home alone
savoring
each moment
just us
Anam Cara
celebrating
with you
from a distance
we are alive
fearless
responsible
considerate
breathe deep
sing
dance
shake
laugh
create
be
grateful
for the ride
what a roller coaster ride
this can be
thank the goddess
my seat belt is fastened
I sweat and shake
on the way up
then let loose

my scream
on the decent
shake
sweat
scream
with each rise and fall
except
when I'm on the ground
big deep belly breath
grounded
earthed
centered
without the craziness
of the ride

13 aug 20

going for that last delicious sip
cream and java
and
coffee grinds

that's a wakeup call
spit it back
from whence it came

when life spits at you
spit back

be grateful
for the opportunity

what I like most about Krishna
is his integrity
he lies too
there are moments in life
when lying is better for
the greater good
than honesty

how to make sense
of paradox

we never know

what we'll be called to do
except
when it happens

be present
forget the past
trust

I mean
can you imagine
trump's head
carved on mt. rushmore
orange hair and all
too much

14 aug 20

15 aug 20

no more seconds
spirit demands
insists
will not stand
being second

before anyone or anything else
gratitude for the presence
of spirit
smiling as I light the candle
for you
your constancy
being completely here
whenever I show up

I tried to cheat you this morning
and write some work related thoughts first
guess what
none of the programs worked
mind you
they're barely functional now
just enough to squeak out these thoughts

god is everywhere
when I open my heart

thank the goddess
she feels better
doctor Monday

16 aug 20

head stuff

where's the heart

that is a seriously good question

when I light the candle
and greet spirit
in this meditation time
a smile
a big toothy smile spreads
and I feel my heart breathe
a deep freeing sigh
smiling on all the world
in this now
drunk with gratitude
for this moment
for this feeling

then I start thinking about
some pressing nonsense
or other
heart contracts

open
closed
where is my heart
choices

be open
in every moment

it's a challenging practice

17 aug 20

the goddess Sekhmet appeared
on my meditation altar

it's her altar really
I light the candle here
and keep my paraphernalia
coffee mug
iphone
glasses
waters of florida
my sacred objects

Sekhmet
healer
heal your beloved

doctor day today

can't write another word
scared
she might need to be
in hospital
I think it's the medication
but then
I have little faith
in pharmaceuticals
especially with a compromised
immune system

18 aug 20

19 aug 20

I missed you yesterday.
no practice.
I put other before you.

I hesitated when I wrote the date
19th
labyrinth walk tonight

I intended to write 18
and write twice today
to make up for my loss
so no one would know
if anyone ever reads this
which is totally unlikely
that I missed a day
except me and thee

If I lie to myself
that's what I offer to the world
gotta ask
what else am I lying to myself about

I can be so distracted
I just answered the phone
my healthcare provider calling
is that more important

than my soul
of course not
body or soul
body and soul

choices
without judgment
just noticing
with compassion
meditation

today is a Knoxville day
recycling is overflowing
gotta get meds
run errands

long day away

20 aug 20

it's all about trust
spirit knows better than me
about what's best for me
and whatever happens
is exactly what's meant to be
for me to grow and learn

if I take what comes
as a slap in the face
if I didn't get what I want
and think
I'm being punished in some way
something wrong about me
not enough
my fault
undeserving
I'll get more of that

if I take what comes
as a gift from the universe
and embrace whatever is
with gratitude
I'll get more of that

with awareness
habitual patterns
offer choices
for doing something different
new neural pathways

this morning
I read about trust
in the Osho Zen Tarot commentary book
page happened to be opened there

you have to take the leap
even with doubt present
if you doubt doubt will grow
if you trust trust will grow
it can be terrifying
to take the first step
come to the edge
said Apollinaire

21 aug 20

empty
nothing's coming out
don't know what I feel
what I want
what's on my mind
not important anyway

what's important
what do I need to write
why do I need to write

honesty
honest me

I could have lied to myself
about writing
then where would I be
as an ally on the path
nowhere
the worst kind of hypocrite

I suppose that's what I've been doing
being all long
until I made the recent
commitment to practice
awareness

I'm not very good at it
that's okay

as long as I practice
I'll get better

in devotional chanting
of the goddess's name
over and over
it is said She will eventually
enter your soul

22 aug 20

life or death
what do I want
what is my legacy
do I care what I leave behind
or to whom
not really
I thought I'd help make
the world a better place
through my work
and I did
I thought I'd do more
but I didn't'
I don't have children
not even close friends
one or two

we own the house
it's a beautiful healing place to live
for us
maybe no more
too much work to maintain
for the 68 and 80 year old women
stewarding this place

I'm a part time cashier at a hardware store
no consequence or meaning to that
except a wage
and not a living one

I have Freedom and Trust
and my Beloved
who no longer calls me that

what do I have to live for

everything

for one
I'm breathing

for everything
each moment is a miracle
a blessing
a magical adventure

spirit has a plan

because I know I belong
regardless of what I do
or who I am in the world
because I am connected
with spirit

halleluyah

23 aug 20

I put Freedom first
my rationale
for putting someone
or something else before You

something expensive on sale
to help ease our Freedom's pain
old kitty limps all the time

it would be on sale after I meditate
so this move is definitely ego

learning about love
respect
integrity

Freedom in the world is hurting

how can I help
how can I ease the suffering

I don't want to feel it now
though I know how suffering feels
I'm more interested in the easing

feel free
grateful
trusting

fearless
responsible
considerate
enjoying each precious moment

if only I learn immediately
from my mistakes

I let my ego slip in
and that's that
enjoy the ride
trusting

24 aug 20

It's taken nearly 20 minutes for the
spinning wheel to stop

ode to a new computer

August 24th
mount Vesuvius erupted in 79 AD
and over 1900 years later
on the same date
spat out my brother

happy birthday

we haven't talked in 10 years now
that's a big ouch
for a retired family therapist

yet it was clearly time to honor
what was
and move on

I suppose I should have
thanked him
for all his betrayals
for helping me see
how I betray myself

and if that's the energy I put out

that's what I get back

gratitude for the insight
doesn't erase
he'd put a wedge between
me and my mum in her final years
encouraged her not to trust me
which we managed to heal
before she crossed
thank the goddess
after her death
he left me some clothes and books
and took everything else
3 full storage units
that's on top of years and years
of other hurtful acts
including incest

at one time
we were the best of friends
we'd addressed and healed
past woundings

I love my brother
I don't like what he's done
may he and his loved ones
be safe and well

curious I even remember

anniversaries

25 aug 20

vacuum whirring
smile
shake my head
attend now
to the whirl of the universe
a song and dance
with stars swirling
into celestial beings
with stories and myth

vacuum
sucks out energy and dirt
the whole time I'm writing
ah
quiet now
space for the new
to emerge

silence
no whirl
yet other hums
in the house
heat pump
water filters
outside
birds
bugs
leaves rustling
in the wind

26 aug 20

so distracted today
no sleep last night
discomfort in neck and shoulder
pins and needles in arms
burning
hurting more laying down
so I got up
and began my day
with things I've needed to do
for ages
felt freeing to be done
yet so much more to do
never ends

sometimes my priorities
are turned around
just notice

the roofer arrived in the middle
of my writing so of course
I stop my practice
he drove an hour and a half to get here
he said the discoloration on the wall
is not a watermark
more a bulge in the sheetrock making a
shadow
he drove an hour and a half for 5 minutes
so glad we don't need to fix anything
on the roof

there is so much to do
to get ready to sell
even if we don't

details details
distract from the silence
the quiet place
restoring
recharging
revitalizing
rest

somedays are like that

all blessed

27 aug 20

remember
falling
in
love

intoxicated

I am
falling in love
with spirit
every breath
every moment
thinking of
You

everything I do
is imbued
with love
with You
in mind and heart

spirit You goddess
what do I call you
Beloved
too long
how about
love
something shorter
an affectionate nick name

for spirit

I don't mean
to be
disrespectful
ever
how can I be affectionate
with an invisible infinity

this is really beyond me
my knowing
through experience

show me
teach me
guide me
be me

is that hubris
yes if coming from ego
no if coming from the true self

28 aug 20

chasing freedom
walk outside this morning
with dog Trust
and feline Freedom
joining

Trust barks and takes off
after some wee creature

Freedom hasn't walked
so much in ages
he's old and gimpy
I hurt seeing how he moves
through space now
ahh aging

Freedom stops and starts
in today's adventure
so is my computer
using voice memos
on my phone

aren't we all chasing freedom
isn't that what being here is all about
to be fully ourselves
to trust explore this amazing world
it's really miraculous
what they find out in science
spectacular connections
body and universe

29 aug 20

Trust walked passed Freedom
through the door
onto the rug
to be rubbed and loved

amazing teachers
when I pay attention

if I cross a boundary
Freedom quickly draws blood
not lately thank goodness
moments later we're friends again

why do humans hold grudges

because we are mostly
not present
we remember woundings
in the past
and fear their repeating
in the future

now what

30 aug 20

I was not a good friend
I listened
empathized
distracted
spoke about me
we stayed in feelings
agitation anger despair disgust

I didn't remember
the bottom of the ocean
still silent peaceful
no matter whatever's storming
on the surface
be it typhoon
tsunami

there is destruction
devastation
loss

out of chaos
creation

what's happening now
is our slow planetary suicide
extinction
some beliefs and practices
definitely need to die
like me thinking

I'm better than you

we are one

what else can we do

live fearlessly
be responsible and considerate
enjoy each precious moment
this too shall pass

31 aug 20

Freedom bit and clawed Mo
36 hours ago
hand so swollen
she's sleeping now
I hope

told not to phone
the local doc
for an appointment
until she sees how she feels
I so want to disrespect
her wishes

write
right
rite

what is going on
larger story

healing crisis
inside and out

Freedom bites and claws
to say no
no more
don't do that
been held down long enough
won't take it anymore

riot in the streets
better to destroy property
than take a life
or is it

I think so
our government doesn't

when profit and property
are more important than people
Freedom bites and claws

I just made that up

I hate violence
hate is violence
I am
what I hate

the point is
love
not violence or fear
is the just response

I would not respond
with physical violence
to Freedom the cat
should he bite or claw me
I might yell or swat the air
I hope

after a few minutes apart

we make up
set new boundaries
sniff each other
gently touch
maybe purr

life goes on

1 sept 2020

night write
not taking out time
with spirit till now
does strain my temperament

I was so short with Mo
even apologized

80th birthday tomorrow
she's not been well
for several months now
local doc today for the bite
the antibiotic for the cat bite
is taking it's toll
tomorrow kidney doc
and her primary
and I'm supposed to cook
steak and lobster

I burn for you
yet
I've not managed
to show you
yet

just being.
here
now
together

is enough

a moment of connection
lagniappe

being with you
cream on the top

2 sept 20

the birth day
months of not being well
and being on retreat
what connection
birth day
doc day
what else to say

heart is still
weary
not energized
as I would have
especially today

perhaps meditating will recharge
perhaps I need a new battery

me and my shadow
me and my computer
now I can no longer
send or receive emails
had to change the DNS
do not resuscitate
and nothing works
maybe tomorrow I'll phone
technical support

today
I'm going for spiritual support

help me stay open and kind
at ease and grateful
loving and respectful
always

3 sept 20

4 sept 20

what happened
to yesterday
no memory

just is
not good or bad

such is life
the past is past
just is
no good or bad
no attachment

what I do with now
counts
nothing else

this practice of righting
writing
is honoring me
my soul

if I don't
honor me
no one else will

how I am with me
is how I treat others
and how I am treated
by others
until I see the mirror
outside reflecting back
how I am with me

a different perspective
on the golden rule
treat my self
as I want to be treated

I treat you the way I treat myself
if I'm judging me
you can bet I judge others
if I'm angry with me
I'll bring anger into my relationships

in this moment
I am
at ease
peaceful
grateful
smiling
breathing deep

a wrinkle in time
moment out of time
now
infinity

eternity
me and ye
one

5 sept 20

4 hours with techies
to get email and internet back

so I went to check on my science project
making plasma water
according to Keshe
gans is energy medicine on steroids
Carolyn's helping me
be a mad scientist

protection in this day and age
my body wisdom said do

project rearranged
flash anger

looking up
I notice
Freedom at the door
perfect timing
he's so intuitive
or spirit is
feel it
lightning
thunder
gone
calm
after the storm

when I own my thoughts and feelings
and let them run their course
my internal weather changes
just like that

like the child
allowed to temper tantrum
without interruption
laughs and cuddles
in the next moment

6 sept 20

whatever the apple techs did
worked
computer is having
temporary health revival
I still can't get email
in two accounts

social isolation
exacerbated
we are each
ultimately
alone

can I live
alone
with myself
my experiences
this one precious life
and feel
peace
ease
love
compassion
bliss
gratitude

if not
I'm living
in illusion

ego created

anything
that interferes
with my connection
with soul
needs to die

bang bang
I shot you dead

all this self hatred
in the world needs to stop
all lives matter
not just black and white

If we were lucky
blessed enough
to be born human
not a creepy crawlie
four legged
or winged one
our life matters

god
goddess
put us here
to remember
and be true
to our source
where we come from
where we're going

one with all

children
often
misunderstand
hurtful experiences
as their fault

as adults
if we don’t realize
that what happened
was the responsibility
of the person who was hurtful
we make ourselves suffer more

if I choose not
to own that
and heal
then
I’ll throw
my hate at you

that’s that

7 sept 20

sometimes I re read
the previous post
distraction from the moment
I allow
rationalizing

as long as I take my time with you
keep my commitment
does it matter when I practice

practice being present
re reading
editing
is past

to be in the present
wait in the silence
see what comes up

the silent voice of spirit
my true self
or ego
talking
how to recognize the difference

8 sept 20

no fire ceremony on the 7th
no energy
nothing to give
not wanting to receive
wanting to be home
in my own energy

existential dilemma
individual or community

my bias

if I'm not giving to me
when I need to
and choose to put
someone or something else first
I won't be giving my best
I'll be holding something back
like I'm doing with myself

spiritual dilemma
trust or fear

if I'm not trusting myself
or more importantly
spirit
I live in fear
if I doubt myself
I doubt the world

I doubt
divine infinite existence

DIE
for short

true
I am more in my head
than heart these days
if I let myself feel
what's happening
I am so incredibly
angry and sad
filled with compassion
and despair
that life and our planet
are so expendable
to make a profit
that it's worse to destroy property
than it is to take a life

violence comes from
self hatred
just stop it
love

9 sept 20

6 minutes left of the 19
to write
thank all the powers that be
and 0% balance transfers
I'm getting a new computer
in a week

lighting
bright rays
between dark clouds
a bit ominous
foreboding
lightning
thunder
I misunderstood
cut grass
I thought she wanted cut
but she didn't
wrath of khan
I asked twice
maybe we were in
a different conversation

10 sept 20

new adventures
make
new neural pathways
anything non habitual
opens a different route
away
from the habit rut
grooves run deeper and deeper
harder to get out of
when so embedded
yet anything
driving to a never visited city
opens the possibility

habits often kill
certainly spontaneity
creative thinking

writing
meditating
stretching
are healthy practices
not habits

why is a nun's dress
called a habit
hmmmm

perhaps wearing

the same something
day in and out
is the habit
like a burka
or
perhaps the habit
is the roving eye
cloth covers
any hint of sexuality

monks and nuns wear similar dress

I need to do some research

11 sept 20

in the middle of the night
ding goes my phone
from sleep
I feel a surge of anger
why does someone send a message
in the middle of the night
then I realize
I'm angry with me
for not figuring out
how to turn the dings off

I think I fixed the settings now

but did I fix them in my life

is the anger I feel really my responsibility
because of something I did or didn't do
easier to be angry at you
than me

surely if anger is like thunder and lightning
it needs full release
before moving on

if anger stays stuck
if I'm stuck in anger
then the feeling turns inward
and hurts only me

grudges limit
like a bad habit
stuck in a rut
inflamed
no connection
no love

heaven
hell
with awareness
my choice

12 sept 20

oh to write

just for the joy of it
see what comes up
from wherever

from ego
there'll be drama
greed violence
from the soul
peace bliss

ah choices
why is it I so often choose drama

habit
to feel alive

like feeling
is living

true
and not true

feeling is a profound part yet
not the only part
we are so much more
than feeling
thinking

doing

infinite realm of possibility

13 sept 20

something smells
maybe a dead creature
bit of distraction
to olfactolocate
rather than write

yet here I am
writing about
whatever comes
to my attention
ego
soul
witness

just before I sat down
to write
I thought of a friend
who is fearful
these days

truly
there is much to be
fearful of
our present administration
and the rise of hatred and division
for starters then there's
viruses violence cancer
global warming extinction
who's counting

why bother thinking that way
think another direction
imagine right now
this present moment
being
somewhere in nature
surrounded by beauty
breathe
come to center
remember

fearing something might happen
is useful initially
to warn us of one possibility
of an infinite range of options

an intuition that something difficult
might happen if I were to enter a place
it's good to trust intuition and not go in

if I don't listen to my gut
and do something dangerous
I need a plan
something that helps me feel more safe

and then
I need to trust spirit
grateful for each precious moment

14 sept 20

I smelled death
something nasty
maybe me

recognition
I found mouse turds

spirit has such a unique
sense of humor
gratitude coyote

lessons
smelling death
don't wash
die
maybe it's
not that simple

what needs to die
is dying

so hard to witness
extinction
so sad
so necessary

with all the abuses
perpetrated
by organized religions

human's relationship with spirit
is estranged
strangled
dying in separation

all part of the divine plan
whatever we are given

trusting and grateful

15 sept 20

good coffee hon
with collagen and peptides
went to the chiropractor
yesterday
good man
good healer
I feel better
less frequent
and not as intense
pins and needles
promoting well being
definitely not wanting to get worse
I needed some structural help
home to bash the tiles
off the counter

never a dull moment

when the job is complete
I shall return for
an adjustment

Deepak's recent meditation
on energy and soul healing
addresses prevention as fear based
I never thought of it like that

in VT I was on the state prevention team
makes so much sense

shift the focus to promoting well being
body mind spirit

16 sept 20

oh so weary waking
this morning
this lifetime

waking

awareness
in this present moment
an infinite array
of choices
my response
my sole responsibility

do I let past experience
or fear of the same reoccurring
in the future
cloud my vision
and influence my decision

clear vision
in the present
anything is possible

"once the decision is clear
the doing is easy" from Runes
new computer arrives today

joy joy

distracted by
things to do today

unlock the gate
2 bags of pot. chloride in the water softener
feed fig tree
weed whack ditch
demolish tile countertops
be with spirit
in every breath

17 sept 20

new computer and doc for Mo
no writing

18 sept 20

demolish the counter

19 sept 20

labyrinth day

for years
we used to host
a monthly community walk
at 19:00
3 years ago
we offered the walk
4 times a year
on the 19th of
April June August October
this year
2020
not a one
Moira's health
has been compromised
since the year's start
combined with
being 80
in the pandemic

not a good mix

this morning
on the 19th
Trust begs
for an adventure
a wee walk

this is the first 19th
I have neglected Her
forgive me
overgrown
boundaries blurred
grasses and dying flowers
aren't we all

my prayers change
somewhat
how I express
so much gratitude
for this one precious life

my life needs to change
my Lowe's time
is limited
thank you spirit
exposed to too many differing
opinions and practices

maybe the people who so adamantly
resist mask wearing
don't want to own the masks
they already wear
a front
different outside
with others than
when alone

transparency
seeing through

no mask

inside and outside
congruent
that's integrity
yes

20 sept 20

tears today
greeting the goddess
just feeling sad

I really don't want to sell or move
Mo does

I'll just have to trust
how spirit works this out

in the transfer
of old computer to new
I lost all my contacts
again

maybe a sign of things to come

everything's a part of everything
anyway
you can be yourself
if you let yourself be

happiness runs
happiness runs

Corinne calls this adjacency
sad and happy next to each other
gratitude and despair
what is our world coming to

extinction
is a slow arduous process

make the best of each moment

and sometimes cry
for the loss
acceptable loss
200000 deaths from covid in the states
millions of creatures dead from global
warming
species going extinct at alarming rates
1000s of acres burned
floods and hurricanes

how to cope with extinction
love fiercely
embrace whatever comes with
profound gratitude
feel the depth of all feelings

this too shall pass

nothing more to say today

21 sept 20

nothing
silence
breath
open

coffee

addiction

I have many

spirit
is my main one and only
whatever helps experience
heights depths breadths
fade
to silence
peace
bliss

when I don't attend fully
to spirit
distracted by ego's dramas
visionary vegetables
always an option
to helps me remember and

stop

every thought
feeling
action
part of ego
the part necessary
to interface with
the illusory outer world

inner world
is another matter
there
true self
soul
resides
eternal
now
no past
or future

in that place
no mind
words clearly limit
and have no place
there
still
peace
anything
everything
possible

breathe in

Today is the first day since I started writing that I forgot to set the timer. Happy Solstice.

22 sept 20

renovating

re nova ting
probably not about
remembering
smoked salmon within

synchronicity
is telling me something
else perhaps about an exploding
astronomical event
new star in the galaxy
something wondrous
happening

amidst utter chaos

in good weather
when the grass is
not too tall and cushy
I do the stretching meditation
on the earth
in the sun
late morning
drops of dew
still sparkle
and tickle wet
on my back
breathe Her in

hugging
being held
breath comes easier
muscles relax
thoughts feelings sensations
disappear
in this place of ease
is grace

earthing

love your Mother

she gives freely
abundantly
until no more is left
then poof
gone
extinct

touch Mother
with profound gratitude
in this moment

y' just never know
what's next

23 sept 20

Freedom's here
he's so psychic

we all are
with
heart and mind
open
free
from judgment
the past
every belief
that separates

what will it take
to clear away old beliefs
that keep us from
our birthright
inner silence
peace
still
bliss
ease
trust
compassion
rejuvenation

words meaningless
without experience

try it
you'll like it

when I think about the world situation
pandemic global warming police killing blacks
hurting and jailing peaceful protesters
I feel indescribable pain despair and shame

it used to be safe to disagree on politics

choices

24 sept 20

nothing present
no
thing
pre
sent

we come in
open
hollow bone
we still are
open
in
silence

whack
smack on the butt
to know I'm alive
I have to take a deep breath
to cry
from the shock
of coming out
into pain and bright lights

outer world
sure can be
a dangerous place
most especially when
I forget
where I came from

and where I'm going
when this life ends

what's present

this amazing journey
next step on the path
labyrinth called life

25 sept 20

after work
cleansing ritual
the shower
hot water
runs
over head
down body
thrilling
to be touched
everywhere
at once
if I so choose

let water and wind
enfold me
let nature
hold me
water
wind
spirit
goddess
god
mother nature
embraces me
like no other

so grateful
to be held
holding you

26 sept 20

what a wild and crazy ride
seatbelts fastened
do I feel viscerally
like I'm holding on
for dear life

do I imagine
from a distance
what being on this wild ride
feels like
perhaps

do I focus attention
somewhere else

choices

aware
witness watches
without
attachment
to whichever
drama ego chooses
to heal

witness
the part inside
each of us
the part that watches

and feels
unconditional
compassion and love

no judgment
toward anyone
or anything

what I hate
in you
is part
of me

27 sept 20

Yom Kippur
begins at dusk tonight
day of atonement
at one men t
on the cross
crossroad

tell me
I need to know

how does
one person
one race of people
learn to believe
they are better
than any other

how is it we learn to disrespect
abuse and violate another human being
another god created creature

so much violence
my way is better than your way

my way is better for me
as your way is better for you
differences enrich
they feel threatening
when I doubt my own way

honor the differences

all meant
to be
here
now

at one men t

28 sept 20

29 sept 20

comparing
is violence
against self

I just had a moment

I've been reading
Chopra Osho and
Joe's latest book
Snake Oil and the Truth
of the Twisted Path

tiny bit of vertigo
spinning realization

we write about similar truths
so differently
Joe's words pull me
waterfall plunge
into the depths
what a thrill

as kids
my brother Andy
and I both played piano

he was really good
I was good
I stopped playing

healing

we need as many
different voices
as possible
to speak
the twisted truth
eventually
every path leads
to the same place
within
we are one

come on people now
smile on each other
everybody get together
try to love one another
right now
right now

(The Youngbloods made the most notable version of this song and these lyrics in 1967. They say smile on your brother; I changed the words.)

30 sept 20

such a thrill
to set the timer
and be able to write
right away

so grateful for
debt financing
and 0% balance transfers

I learned patience
with the old one
I could spend
my precious moments
waiting
feeling irritated
wasting time or perhaps
feeling grateful
enjoying having absolutely
nothing to do

with the new one
I'm able to do so much more
in much less time

for that I am
equally grateful

not today
spirit has other plans

as of 4 this morning
when I woke
there was no internet wifi or phone
there won't be for a bit
out in the world stuff is stymied
unless I drive half an hour to town
that's not happening

many plans for today
upended

laughter is
the best medicine

when coyote comes
gotta love 'em
embrace the moment
anything less
isn't trusting
spirit knows best

1 October 20

so much hangs
on this coming election
and yet
on some level
nothing will change
other than I might be
able to breathe
a bit easier
when our current administration
is toppled
if it isn't
I'll have to breathe
a bit deeper

my work is still the same
no matter what drama
is happening on the outside
my work
be
love
compassion
light
wherever I am
whomever I'm with

that's an inside job
peeling away
everything that distracts
and interferes with

remembering
core connection
heart and soul
how blessed
I am
to be in this moment
alive

this is the first year
since March in 25 that
we've not had one guest
here for healing

reclaiming home

2 oct 20

spirit has her ways

president and first lady got it
the virus
covid
one month before the election
spin
world turns
next direction
in the medicine wheel

it is such a challenge to stay
in spirit
with all the drama
these days

bring out the best and the worst
of me

my first reaction was
good
inevitable of course
even money and power
don't offer protection
when it comes
to the invisible

spirit has her ways
trusting whatever's meant to be

most other heads of state
have survived
had money and resources
to buy the necessary care

I hope he doesn't deteriorate more mentally
his thinking could really short circuit

prayers and energy for
best possible outcome

in spirit's hands
what if it's a hoax
and he's doing it to disappear
so he needn't lose face
maybe he'll move to Russia

I have ancestry in Russke
and Germany

I'm just gonna sit back
and watch

witness seer storyteller

3 oct 20

hungry
berries and cream
smushed
sweet
mmmm

lovely way
to start the day
I eat so the goddess
can taste her exquisite creation
then savor a sip of java
for Krishna's pleasure and delight

simple ways to give back
eating with awareness
eating for the goddess
for all vision questors
without food
for all souls
who hunger

slowly slowly slowly
I learn to quiet thinking
I watch me thinking
chant the mantra
stop
start thinking
again
practice

no thinking
empty mind
infinite realms of possibility

new addition
to the practice
begun last week
remember the mantra
at bedtime
I've not yet managed once

so much for awareness
practice
teaching what I need to learn

4 oct 20

morning chores complete
perfect timing
8am practice
as I light the candle
and greet the goddess
I offer my gratitude and love
I notice with the
slightest shift of stance
more aches
than before

I've scrimped on my
physical stretching time
body needs more care

if what is out there
what I attend to
is a mirror
of what's present in here
then the goddess must be aching
clearly she needs more care

I can change the ending
of the story to anything I want
infinite realm of possibility

realm of infinite possibility
R I P for short
rest in peace

without a body
R I P

with a body
being in this existence
means needing an
ego
mixed blessing
each thought feeling action
can bring me
to greater connection or separation
with spirit
choices

5 oct 20

from the beginning
of this practice
I've used the timer chimes
on the iphone

today
with insight timer
Tibetan bowls
3 chimes
begin and end
these 19 minutes
pen to page

what exactly
is this practice

listen to silence
write whatever comes
trust whatever comes
from that still place
going deeper into soul
unconditional compassion
smash the mirror
honor time boundaries
start and stop on the bell
do what I say I'll do

if I don't practice
what I teach

I lie to myself

if I lie to me
you can bet
I'll lie to you

what is spiritual practice

we are one

6 oct 20

the way I see it
if we're here
born into a body
we have an
unalienable right
to be here
god chose us
god knows better

I don't have the right
to take someone's life
because I have nothing better to do
because I'm feeling threatened
angry
because I hate me
because I'm feeling so miserable
because I make myself feel this way

easier to blame you

If I judge me
I judge you

I need to take responsibility
for how I judge myself
become aware
honor
release
grow compassion

and stop it

it starts with what we do to ourselves
not what was done to us

children make sense of what grown-ups do
as children do
everything revolves around them
when trauma happens
child believes s/he
must've caused it

as children age
we learn what happened to us
had nothing to do with who we really are

7 oct 20

8 oct 20

so easy to let outside take priority
over spiritual practice
choose to do things
that need doing
instead of
meditating
feeling free
eternally
infinitely

loving spirit above all
fills to overflowing

anything less
creates obstacles on the path

don’t get me wrong
existence brings challenging
if not traumatic experiences
because we can heal
whatever old wounds
need healing
existence says
here
deal with it

because you can
trust me

that's the point
when I
trust spirit
whatever spirit brings
life is peace joy bliss

when I question
why me
and doubt spirit
when I push the river
try to change course
and direct the flow
outer life is stress and anxiety

9 oct 20

lodge dismantled
ceremonial fire lit
prayers for
patience gratitude healing
willow is ready to return to earth
we burned twine
that bound branches
cut the arched boughs
and gathered bundles
for those who were here

grandmothers and one grandfather
built it
one year ago later this month
in a thunderstorm
spectacular feat

envisioning the impossible
I'm possible
everything is
when I trust

10 oct 20

in that moment
when I light the candle
and greet spirit
a smile beams
across my face
into my heart
and melts

that hardened place
girded to fend off feeling
or perhaps simply
curiously accepting

love in matter
can hurt real bad

wanting something
from another person
that only spirit can give
is a set up
for conflict
separation
and stress

may
the love
I feel
in that moment
of greeting
the goddess

when smile melts heart

be in every breath
I take

hardened
was the word
that came to me
to write on
this morning

is my heart hardened
to this traumatic world we live in
so much awful stuff
I'd be blithering
if I let myself feel

once on a meditation walk
by a sweet peaceful lake in NH
a cigarette butt and beer can
crossed my path
I sobbed inconsolably
non-stop for three hours

in the midst
of all the trauma
in the core

magic
beauty
bliss

11 oct 20

just start writing
away from thoughts spinning
still I run from you
thinking
I need to write
something else
instead of a love letter
to you

maybe
everything I write
is a love letter
even when it comes
through ego

if only
I could be
that aware

maybe I am
and simply forgot
as I learned
in the school of life
that what seems real
isn't
and what isn't seen
is

remembering

12 oct 20

the hum of silence
can be deafening

thoughts	still
feelings	wide open
actions	anything's possible

nothing more to say

hummmmmm

birthright

where we come from
what we come in with
where we return

yet the world
society
religion
government
family
mostly
tell us something different
that we are separate
and need more
like filling a bowl
with a very big hole

forgetting
our connection
with source

we are holy
whole
one with all

being empty
full of possibility

birthright

13 oct 20

14 oct 20

what happened to yesterday
gone
in a flash
missed opportunity
to sit alone quietly with you
just us
breathing together

fess up Jo
yesterday
I walked the labyrinth
after publishing
our community rag

the fess up part
I walk maybe once a month
when the call consumes
she's so overgrown
unkempt
wild

I've never let her
winter over like this
always trimmed for the cold
maybe this winter she'll be warmer

though feet mostly remember
I stumble on the path
frequently
and
on this this day
of all the days I walk
oyster mushrooms
on the path

the goddess is so good to me

lessons
trust the timing
spirit is
unconditional
generosity
compassion
love and understanding

no judgment
no comparison
no guilt
no shame
all imposed from outside
not real feelings

15 oct 20

so different
Trust wanted desperately to walk
so today
write and meditate
creekside

dog's wandered off
alone

now I see Trust
digging for buried treasure

everywhere in nature

with this silly iphone
write in notes
timer in insight timer
Deepak's teachings in his app
what else could I possibly need

Trust sat by my side as I wrote
that last line

trust is what I need

today
chariot drives to Asheville
insidiously stressful
don't say a thing

lips sealed

trust in silence
all will be revealed

16 oct 20

best report yet
phew

so powerful
thoughts and chemicals

medical and pharmaceutical
agriculture and oil industries
want us to stay sick
so they make money more money

if we don't buy in
don't believe in
the fear they spread
they shrink and we get healthy

let's all get healthy

breathe deep
I release all toxic beliefs
that belittle me
I claim my place
in the infinite realm
of possibility

17 oct 20

hummm
of heat pump reminds me
in Sanskrit
hum is
I am
vibration of sound
remembers

fan's off

hum
in greater silence

driving home from work
last night
within a mile
fox darted across the road
clear in the headlights
less than 10 seconds
skunk waddled in tall grass
within a minute
deer sighting by the old pond
day before
black snake slithered

so blessed
spirit wants to tell me something
totems
omens

signals from the goddess
fox medicine
wily hidden playful fierce
skunk
very clear about boundaries
respect
deer
gentle loving generous
snake
shedding skins transformation
death rebirth

18 oct 20

headed for extinction
clearly set
on destruction
fear and greed
spread by
doubt and hatred

that's the virus

that's the future

how do I live fully
in the present

trust and generosity
awareness
thinking
feeling
doing
aligned

I am in charge of me
I control nothing else
how I respond to a situation or event
is up to me
my soul responsibility

as an adult

as a child
I'm sorting through everything
trying to make sense of the world around me
and believing everything around me
is because of me
as I get older
that turns into
my fault
I start to not trust me
and the spiral continues from there

as an adult
until I remember
who I am
not others' images and
expectations of me
I am responsible
for continuing to believe
others' stories about me
I am responsible
for selling my soul

19 oct 20

labyrinth walk tonight at 19:00
19 is definitely
a favored number

greeting the goddess
this morning

I so wish
I could hold You
the way You hold me
all over
every bit of me
exposed to You
Your breath
the air enfolds me
like no other
immersed
into waters' caress
all over
everywhere
almost drowned
yet buoyed by Her touch

uplifted
blessed

still
I often run
from being with Her

ego adventure
of some sort
distracted by another silly thought

life
love

becoming more aware
each day

speaking of water and distractions
the phone just rang
and I answered it
left the practice for outside contact
yup
plumber's coming to
disconnect the kitchen sink
to be reconnected
after the election

glad I did
they were not told
GPS to our address
gets you lost

I'll have time to write
not meditate before
they arrive
auch well...

20 oct 20

something this morning
said meditate first
shake it up
be bold
do something
non habitual

so I did

now look what you've done
opened to the infinite
realm of possibilities

anything out of the ordinary
non habitual
creates new neural pathways

we have an imPOTUS
who's decompensating
ripples from the top

I ask myself
how am I the same
how am I different
how can I grow more compassion
trust and gratitude
for this one precious moment

events outside

make it more difficult
to trust anything
except
our own experience

so many jewels
in the garbage
sift what's useful
throw the rest away

21 oct 20

did you ever feel
so much love in your heart
that you might explode
in joy
awe
wonder

in that moment
of being seen
heard
loved
by another
4 legged
2 legged
sunrise
Yosemite
I remember
the feeling
exploding
inside me
core of who
I am

when spirit enters form
we forget
where we came from
what's in us
where we return

the act of being born
is so shocking
we forget how we got here
and everything we embodied
before we had a body

politics society
organized religion
encourage us to forget
to give our soul away
become a commodity
so “they” can have more

don’t listen to them

listen to heart and soul
trust intuition
put self first
take care
like only I can
body heart mind
soul

22 oct 20

old white men
jerking off
looking at pictures
of little children
and their power
over others

how did they get to be
so scared and angry
unconscious of their own self hatred
violence projected out
at anything or anyone different
because that
threatens belief
foundations crumble

I'll tell you how

buying into the material world
selling soul
buying into what they say

not listening to intuition
not trusting soul and spirit above all else

I came in
to the universe
as a gift
of love

from spirit

I entered the world
with spirit's love

how did I learn
to lose
the core of me

even more important
how do I find and open
again to the love within

everything I've ever done
in my life
got me
to now
to this moment
this awareness

grateful for it all

23 oct 20

Tibetan bowl tones
vibrate awake

unconditional compassion
and forgiveness
for self
heals
self hatred

no one can do that for us

it's an inside job
probably
why we came here
in the first place

it's so easy
to get distracted
and run to explore
another avenue
to feed insatiable ego

it's so easy

when we
work within
for unity
an end to divisiveness
self judgment and comparison

learned from past experience

necessary then
tattered remnants now
no longer useful

let past be past
be present

this moment
without prescribed
thought feeling action
is wide open
infinite possibility

as more and more
threats to our civil rights grow
with more and more to fear
happening outside
which I have absolutely
no control over
I could become
anything
blithering idiot
non violent activist
ostrich
love and compassion

how I choose to respond
is up to me

my responsibility

24 oct 20

up too early
4:30 am
work at 8
rambling

David and Goliath
child takes down giant
with slingshot
miracles happen

let this be the miracle
little person
slays ego
slingshot is
awareness

wake up

I lost faith
in organized religion
this is the only way
through me
lie
along with all the
sexual abuse of children

I need
direct relationship
with god
not an intercessor

25 oct 20

where to begin

I take a sip
for Krishna
let this body
experience the thrill
for him
Krishna doesn't have a physical body now
he has an infinite realm of possibilibodies
all his
I am a tiny weeny itsy bitsy part of spirit
spirit is all of me

I used to be swelled headed
hubris they call it
thinking god is in me
and I can do anything

that's only true
when what I want is in alignment
with spirit's plan for me

when I get ego out of the way
and embrace whatever comes
like a lover
coming home
to her beloved

trust trumps fear

that was an intentional choice of word

they are spinning fear
don't buy into it

buy into trust
intuition and spirit

give a gift
get present
just do it

postscript
I first met Krishna
in Osho's Transformational Tarot
healing parables from different
cultures and religions
I chose the card "play"

26 oct 20

Osho tells the story
in the bhagava gita
a conversation between
Krishna and Arjuna

millions of soldiers
prepare for battle
first cousins
go to war
rivers of blood

Arjuna is high command
for the good guys
Krishna is his chariot driver
"ride out"
let's look
at what's about to take place
Krishna obeys

surveying throngs of warriors
both sides
Arjuna has a panic attack
wants to call off the war
killing loved ones mentors friends
is not worth it

Krishna tells Arjuna
to experience the fullness
of who he is

spiritual warrior
they discuss
how the outcome
already decided
is not in our hands

so play

without
attachment to outcome
your life depends on it
warrior
life on the line
with every breath

27 oct 20

sitting in silence
words float by
nothing grounds

like coffee grounds

take a sip
for Krishna

open to now

so many different ways
to name the un nameable
naming spirit
limits
the limitless

ah paradox

how to embrace
all that is
light and dark
black and white
all color in between

how to feel gratitude
this one precious life
in a body with
full sensory visceral experience

so easy to forget
our sixth sense
intuition

world outside
has gone crazy
divided divisive deluded

in that quiet place
inside silence
I find my truth
what's right for me
not for anyone else

not my responsibility
I am

when I listen and take on
someone else's truth
as my own
I give my power away

to thine own self
heart
soul
be true

28 oct 20

editing

sometimes
I just
leave words
as they're written

sometimes
I edit

raw or refined
me

if I judge myself
in any way
for whatever
I say
or do
or think
I betray spirit
and me

mistakes
adventures in learning
learn

it is
the meaning I make
from experience

that brings me joy
or suffering
not the experience

how I make sense of things
can keep me trapped
or free me

choices

in ego
trapped

in soul
free

grateful for
each precious moment

as simple
as turning on
a light switch
flip the lever

choose awareness
come home

29 oct 20

high noon
and you are here
with me
whenever
it's convenient
for me --
noon
first thing in the morning
dusk
before bed
I may not even show up at all
and yet
you are here
for me
anytime
anywhere
whenever I'm ready
whenever I make time

only the goddess can do that
happy to see me whenever

I'm so blessed

funny thing is
we all are
blessed
when we open
love

within

connection
everywhere
one with all

hurricanes batter
glaciers melt
seas rise
fire consumes
nature
enraged
by our collective trashing
pillaging
raping
the gifts she gives

love the earth
as we love ourselves
as we love spirit

perhaps the way we treat the earth
is the way we treat ourselves
everything mirrors
till we
smash the mirror

30 oct 20

another room
writing
waiting
for Joe
and a cuppa

together
we drink to Krishna
and the Goddess
drinking spirits
gets me high
whoever
we toast

how to be safe
with my brother
whom I've not seen
really in ages
besides once
briefly
fire ceremony

to hug or not to hug
wear a mask
stay 6 feet apart
be the way we were
pre pandemic

every choice

life or death
how or when
is already decided

how to be
true
to me
heart
soul
spirit

in between
now and then

for a moment
I forget

run away
live an entire new life
and return
without
the glass of water

a seeker finally meets god
in the desert
before he can speak
god says
will you get me a glass of water
there's a village just yonder

seeker knocks on the first door
falls in love with the woman who opens it

marries
has 3 children
successful business
and 12 years later
a flood comes and wipes out the village
everything everyone
except the seeker
drowned
he finds himself in the desert
he sees
god
and
before he can speak
god says
did you bring my glass of water

31 oct 20

what kind of masks
for today
Halloween
I'll wear Darth
at the register
at lowe's

register love
respect differences

why feel and act
more important
than another living being

if I'm threatening myself
by believing and feeling
I'm less important
unworthy

foundations
old beliefs
crack and crumble
fade away

sacred present
arises
in consciousness
we are one

breathe
love
compassion
gratitude

coldest night yet
first real frost
sparkles
as it melts
and burns
delicate growth
end of season

the wheel turns
I can meditate
anywhere
musical rooms

when I opened the door
to greet the morning and see and feel
what's what
Trust popped her head out of her house
and I invited her in

Trust walked right in
miracles happen

1 November 20

what a year
what a week

2020 election week
historical
hysterical

hysteria
in the old days of psychology
when woman was labelled hysterical
it was thought
she had a
wandering uterus
that found its way
say to an arm
which became numb

that's how they explained symptoms
they couldn't explain

apt perhaps for this time
uteruses wandering
not feeling home
not belonging
because
society denies sovereignty

especially for women
though not just

the right to choose
life or death
my body
my choice

taking my own life
is a crime
beginning and end of life
or anywhere in between
why

whatever is growing
inside me
is my responsibility
my decision
my body
virus
bacteria
organs
fetus
my body
my choice

imagine women's sovereignty
fully restored
heaven on earth

how I treat myself
is how I treat others
if I am enraged about abortion
how am I not allowing something new

to be born in me

instead of
honoring and uplifting
our differences

we try to change each other
sometimes kill
out of fear
doubt
self hatred

time to stop
remember
we are one

everything
is a choice

2 nov 20

cuddling Freedom
ole kitty
he came downstairs
to meditate with me
I said to myself
if he comes over
I'll ask if he'd like me
to pick him up
put him on my lap

he did
what a momentary blessing

feral kitties
carry DNA
of the wild
tend not to sit
on any laps
so I'm told

Freedom stayed
for a wee bit
he didn't draw blood
just moved
indicated he wanted down

seeing his difficulty moving
I ever so gently
place him on the ground

still both hind legs flop over
he stays there for a moment
flopped over

selfish of me
loving Freedom so

next time
pillow first
then very carefully
seat the Beloved

holding Freedom
even for one fleeting moment
is the blessing of a lifetime

that feeling inside
is inside me
outside experiences
may help me remember
awaken bliss
the feeling is in me
is me

help me learn about love

3 nov 20

election day
I love Donald Trump
I never thought I'd say that

he's put either/or
duality
writ large
in the faces
of the whole wide world
almost mythic
definitely comic
totally tragic
to witness
self hatred
so externalized

gotta love him
or be him
he spews hate

love
unity
compassion
trust in spirit
heart and soul
intuition
come home
remember

Donald reminds us
how far away we've gone
he is the epitome
of self hatred
with power
hmmm
who else do we know
like that

I am you
and you are me
and we are all
together

I hate to admit it

that's the problem

so I go blind
to what I don't like
in myself
and see that in you

learning to no longer love self
maybe helped me survive
when I first learned to do so

guess what

it's not true
it's a lie
let that foundation crumble

we are love
inside
invisible foundation
who we are

if we were taught
as children that
everything we experience
only happens
to help us learn
about how
to love ourselves
even more
in challenging situations

nothing that happened to us
is our fault
the meaning we make
out of what happened
is
our responsibility

4 nov 20

our country is so divided
mirroring what's going on inside
each soul on the planet
in some way
or it wouldn't be happening

no clear winner yet

sometimes
I'm so eager to sit
and write
I forget
to light the candle
and love on
the goddess
for a brief moment
feel gratitude
blessed
in every cell
with every breath
for this one precious moment

we came here to be love
anything less is
drama ego creates
illusion

nothing to do
with who

we really are

paradox

drama
separates us and
at the same time
points the way back
home
connection

self hatred
ends
now

5 nov 20

bear came last night
Trust had that loud steady protective bark
and was close
so with tactical flashlight in hand
I point near the dog
two golden orbs
shone back at me
then dark shape
emerges
we look at each other
no turning away

transmission

fearless
curious
holding ground
too close to home
for Trust
she seemed most threatening
constantly communicating
keep your distance
from my loved ones

thank goodness
for social distancing
with the animal kingdom

best look up bear medicine

spirit wants me to understand something
about this moment

still no result
no landslide election
so close

Greek theater
players then wore masks
everyone
the whole wide world
is watching
the fight between good and evil
fear and trust

6 nov 20

table's too high
chair too low
uncomfortable writing here
in this room
physical distraction

what do I need
to feel more comfortable
here right now

after several adjustments
words tiptoe out these fingers

19 minute writing meditation

what joy
creating
lines on a page
scribbles
whether anyone else
ever reads a word
for me and thee
just for fun

write me
tap the keys
that tell this story
I know you are

I just don't always give you credit
or say thank you
I am so amazingly grateful
you are in my life
whatever I name you
limits you
shhh

you are all of me
I am a tiny weenie miniscule part of you
I have to share you
with all the zillions
of other beings
in the universe

7 nov 20

fire ceremony tonight
there in spirit
we're having our own
fire ceremony
at the healing wheel
where our lodge once stood
ghost images waver
grandmothers gathered
one stormy Samhain
one god in hiding helped

against the odds and weather gods
sweat lodge appeared
fire and rain
obstacles on the path

energy is different
with male presence
how am I different

too easy to give my power away
let the man do it
while I watch or do something else

next time
only goddesses

8 nov 20

scratching the surface

I cut my cabbage for sauerkraut
on the corian table
rough edges
need sanding

how can I go deeper
what's rough about me
that needs smoothing

everything is
meant to grow love
even if it doesn't seem so
on the surface

7 nov 20 edited

fire ceremony tonight
with you in spirit

we're having our own
fire ceremony
at the healing wheel
where our lodge once stood

we ceremonially dismantled
the lodge on 19 October
cut willows
made bundles of 13

ghost images waver
grandmothers gathered
one stormy Samhain
one god in hiding helped

against the odds and weather gods
sweat lodge appeared
fire and rain
obstacles on the path
our circle centers

energy is different
with male presence
how am I different

too easy to give my power away

let the man do it
while I watch or do something else
too easy to not speak my truth

how else do I give my power away
how do I sell my soul

how do I do that with you

I cannot change what I'm not aware of

ancient patterns
learned
can be unlearned
with awareness

there was a time
long before
when all goddesses were recognized
and honored

remember

blown away
13 grandmothers
pandemic
retreat

next time
only goddesses

9 nov 20

grandmothers
goddesses
same difference
old hag at the well
offers her magic
and shakes souls
awake

wake up

being together
without ego
celebrating
honoring
being
for ourselves first
then each other
what we gift our world
is the dream
grows the vision
heals

this time of greater social isolation
pandemic virus of hatred and fear
is a magnificent opportunity to be
on retreat a vision quest be with
soul and god

10 nov 20

up up and away
fifth dimension
wasn't that the name of the group
in the 60s
tune in head
I ponder

what is the fifth dimension
where gravity and electromagnetic force
are unified
spacetime fabric
where holograms are possible

head stuff
if I cut a tiny piece of a hologram
and enlarge it
the piece becomes whole
exactly as before the cut
the whole is in each part
brilliant
metaphor
and manifestation
of spirit

another larger story example
we are one

each precious part
of this body is a miracle

to be revered
body needs exquisite care
temple of the soul

how I
experience external events
decides my stress level
and if I don't go with the flow
make meaning
that takes me away from love
I suffer more
and eventually
get sick

11 nov 20

early up
still dark
wet outside
no coffee
my my
inside
still
empty
breathe

okay this is really heady
not yet in my experience

everything's a mirror
space
stars
galaxies
universe
black holes
infinite realm of possibilities
in me
I am a hologram
if I am a tiny weenie cut off
piece of spirit
enlarge me
what now

12 nov 20

autumn
after an all day heavy rain
creek rumbles loud

seasons change
nature in process
of dying
death is so beautiful

walking the same path
with Trust
each day
seeing something new
opening up
to this one precious moment

this year so far
over 230,000 Americans have died
from covid 19
1,290,000 in the world

about 650,000 a year from heart disease
17,900,000 worldwide

over 600,000 of us die from cancer
9,500,000 worldwide

we're gonna die
one way or the other

perspective

why are they trying to scare us so
control
power

now
more than ever
we need to trust ourselves
and spirit
take exquisite care

Friday the 13th nov 20

beautiful day to save lives
beautiful day to die
we've been binging
on Grey's Anatomy
shepherd says to save lives
indigenous people say
a beautiful day to die

a beautiful day to
sit still
watch the sun
enlighten everything
lighten up
what's more important than love

life

I don't think so

just realized
I didn't set the gongs
all this lagniappe time
to write
because I was
careless
about boundaries
a mixed blessing

I wasn't mindful

of the practice
light a candle
greet the goddess
beaming with gratitude
then set insight timer
write

respecting boundaries
around time
and money
trusting whatever happens
being true to my word
doing what I say I'll do
are ways I show love

I got so angry last night
so impatient
with this renovation

I need to renovate myself
and it's taking so long

14 nov 20

healing field of Sophia
I read Peggy Rubin's post
earlier
goddess of joy
love and service

feel falling in love
remember every moment
bliss
peace
gratitude
our birthright

anything that takes me away
from that experience
is illusion

drama
I create
in the material world
to help me remember
to go inside
to the imaginal
invisible
infinite realm
of possibilities
where
bliss
peace

gratitude
abide always

here’s a kicker
I just realized
I forgot to set the timer
again
though I happened
to look at the clock
when I started
and the moment
I remembered I forgot
was 19 minutes
inner gong chimes

15 nov 20

so distracted this morning
flash of
Brooke Medicine Eagle
in an email
interested
I clicked the link
before knowing it
and swiftly fell down
the rabbit hole

I signed up
for the talk
tomorrow

future
or past
thoughts
I feel my neck
muscles tense

brand new now
breathing free and easy

when
I judge or compare
or make light of
anything I do that
separates me
from love

and then with
awareness
notice
with compassion
without judgment
healing happens

now I laugh when I see
how unconscious
I can be

dinna fash lassie
be happy
be love

16 nov 20

it gets better
or worse
depending on one's perspective

in my mind
yesterday
I opened the garage door
in practice
I backed into it

smashed the bugger
have to replace 5 panels

there goes my tax return

I've been asking
spirit for help
opening doors for me

today I fessed up
took responsibility
said I'd replace it

Mo started judging
laying into me
I said "you're cruel"
she agreed and said "I am"
"I don't need to listen to this"
I said and left

that was an open door
at least a new one
I walked right through

grateful for that

blessings in disguise

it's funny
to me
it's only money
granted
I don't have any
I'll come up with it
somehow

maybe
in addition to asking spirit
I need
to open some doors
for myself

a little more mindfully

in the back of my mind
I wonder
if something
is jiggling
out of place
synapses not firing
the way they should
oh well

whatever will be
will be

grateful
it's only the door
not the building

17 nov 20

another day
not having information
about cost
money worries
crop into consciousness
imagining the worst
only hurts me

nothing I can do
except be present
and enjoy
each precious moment

cause ya just never know
when it's time
for the unknown
to surface
from the depths

spirit has a terrific
sense of humor

daily cases of covid
in TN over 7000
yesterday

I'm not laughing
more sad
people can be so inconsiderate

out in public
wear a mask
keep 6 feet apart
cough or sneeze into elbow
wash hands

common sense
things we can do
to stop the spread
of this virus
ego
greed
pride
self hatred

18 nov 20

cold outside
I left the door open
and called

Trust came in last night

such a thrill

to be wild
thrive in the elements
this time of year
frost
bluster
downpour
raw
ahhh
to be free
alive
adventuring
protecting
eating
dry shelter if I need it
the best part
being welcomed inside
with the humans
warmth
love
affection

what a life

dog mirror god
who doesn't want
freedom
to be
true to the wild self

whatever I believe
that limits
my own freedom
to be
is ego
drama
illusion
a lie
I'm choosing to believe

why would I
do something
that harms me

more importantly
what do I need
to help me
choose something
healthier

the bell

19 nov 20

the bell
begin again
each day
each breath
new
unknown
anything is possible
without past belief
or future concern
in the present
the gift
infinite realm
here
now
within

stop thinking
stop feeling
stop doing
just be

just

trusting
spirit
gives
me
what I can deal with
never more

that's faith
good or bad
whatever comes
grateful for each precious moment

driving into the garage door
still gives me pause
wondering about the larger story
clearly being more mindful
is part of the lesson

I need to create
a vacuum
in order to fill it
so I siphon off financial resources
I don't have
for a new garage door
bigger vacuum
bigger fill

secret of happiness
wanting what I have

20 nov 20

glasses off
help me see
with soft eyes
through the mist
invisible realms
begin to materialize

I've never been able to see
only bridge here and there
I know Avalon
with everything in me

once adventuring in Scotland
at the fairy glen on Skye
with dear friends
who see and feel the magic
it's exquisitely beautiful
I ask "do you see any fairies"

just then
wind blusters in
from the west
tall grasses
bend into the wind

do you see them

friends laugh
signs are everywhere

when I pay attention

miracles everywhere
when I pay attention

I've been distracted
attending to thoughts
having nothing to do with
here and now

not knowing how
it will work out
and fretting over it
is not trusting

fretting about an unknown future
when that's all there is
the great unknown
is me
suffering over my suffering

life on earth is challenging
natural disasters happen
all the time
human disasters happen
even more frequently

trust connection
with source
soul intuition

21 nov 20

if I only eat once a day
that's more
than 690 million hungry people
out of 7.8 trillion in the world
that's just wrong

how did this planet tilt so
spin off its axis
why can't the world come together
and be respectful
of differences

why do we need war
the obvious is
it's a money maker

not so obvious is
external conflict
mirrors the war within
between head and heart
belief and faith
fear and trust

why did I start there
noticing a few rumblings
in my tummy
I can't imagine
what starving feels like

I don't want to

22 nov 20

magnificent dawn
red sky this morning
sailor's warning
snail trails
on windowpane
six feet up

how is it possible

so much beauty
magic
I miss
when I'm thinking
about something else

thinking distracts
focus on not thinking

not thinking
is meditation

nothing
going on
except
this
one
precious
moment

breathe

grateful

I can die at peace

grateful

this
one
precious
moment

seems like a good place to stop

23 nov 20

distracted
thoughts of future work

muse me

da muse
she come
when I ask

feel her pulse
in me

creative expression
is essential
for the soul
all the time
especially now

I like to write
take pictures
sing
drum

you

on my bucket list
sing in a black gospel choir
omg
what a thrill

one never knows

what a treasure to take
this time
for whatever
needs
to surface
sit quietly
wait
though
not always
quiet in my mind
for fingers
to move
give expression
to the thoughts
inside
because
they're there

what's more important

human life
or money

without moral compass
probably depends where you sit
on the income spectrum

everything
out there
is distraction

and a way back
into soul

choices
(I forgot the timer)

24 nov 20

afternoon
I took care of business
this morning

by the time it's all done
we will have been
without a kitchen sink
for four months
when the new counter
is finally installed
what a pain in the buttski

counter comes December 28
sink reconnected on the 29th
backsplash up
the following week
boring necessary details
still so much to do
to be ready

spiritually
always ready
for the call
even if I'm doing the calling

practice respect
presence
gratitude
compassion

in every
encounter

sometimes
at home
ego gets tangled
and I don't
I growl

growling is a respectful way
to express anger
doesn't hurt anyone
tone words and body language
can hurt
sometimes I use
hurtful words and tone
I suppose
when I'm feeling hurt
I hurt back

someday
I'll say "ouch that hurts"
instead of acting out
kid part of me
doesn't turn the other cheek

maybe someday
maybe not

25 nov 20

precocious
already feeling grateful
tomorrow is
thanksgiving

I am so incredibly grateful
that indigenous peoples everywhere
survived white perpetrated genocide
so grateful
the people
remember
ceremonies
traditions
language
way of life
one with all
mitakuye oyasin

sounds of silence

door open
cool blast
no human sounds
only the elements

winds dance with oaks
evergreen and pear
leaves rattle into life
whooossshhh

honing in
each tree
sounds different
leaf orchestra
squall whips air
new note in the universe
creek
steady
in the distance
no birds today
too blustery

grateful for the conductor

26 nov 20

thanksgiving day 2020
long pause

how am I grateful
for all unnecessary death
grief
isolation
fear
stress
trauma
that comes with covid

this is how

life in a body on earth
is so amazingly precious

Tibetan Buddhists say
being born human
is more rare
than throwing a life buoy
in the middle of the Pacific Ocean
and having the largest
grandest tortoise
in the ocean
swim its head
into the buoy

I could have been

born a flea

going to die
one way or another

with all the mixed messages
about how to be safe
comes confusion
terrific trance state
open for suggestion

in my face
and consciousness
the question looms
everyday
who do I trust

the only answer

spirit and me
intuition
body wisdom
synchronicity

in the face
of new threats
and the infinite realm
of possibility
I want to
live each moment
present
I'm going to die

one way or the other

how do I want to live

fearless
trusting
spirit and me

27 nov 20

guidelines
for being human

respect boundaries
no means no
when that isn't what
I want to hear or
when I'm confused
about the boundary
I sometimes push
verbally
never physically
by the third no
I get it

grow trust
if I say I'm going to do something
I do it
if I say I'll be there in 5 minutes
and I won't make it on time
I communicate I'll be late
I need more time
I don't just take the time
unless there's an emergency
then I apologize
if you tell me something about you
I keep that knowing close to my heart
I don't tell your story to anyone else
without your permission

ask permission
when I want to touch someone
wait for an answer
are you open to a hug
may I put my hand on your back
can I hold you
when someone's having big feelings
sobbing say
hold the space
not the person
touch interrupts the process
and shifts the focus
to sensation

28 nov 20

church bells toll
vibrations mesmerize
colored tones
shake my soul
the sound of the gong
the death of Quasimodo
I googled the correct spelling
searching for Hunchback of Notre Dame
top of the list
Disney's 1996 cartoon version
not the 1939 classic
with Charles Laughton and Maureen O'Hara
then came the original
novel 1831 by Victor Hugo
the internet is changing history
the number of hits
puts you at the top

how is history being taught

will future generations
remember the holocaust
will 2020 be remembered
for the US almost going into
a dictatorship
and killing 250,000
war in America
negligence and failure to lead
self hatred

29 nov 20

sometimes the computer is smarter
than me
I accidently press some command
the printing changes
and I don't know how
to get back
to before

isn't that shift
spirit's breath

feel the moment
embrace every silly little thing
as a gift from spirit

embrace the change
whatever spirit brings
every experience
is an opportunity
to learn
more about
love
how we love ourselves
honor the divine within
is how we treat others
and how we are treated

if I judge myself
compare

mock
call myself names
I am not loving me

the true self
is the start
adventure of a lifetime
energy into matter
spirit into form
you and me

goal is
love self
the way I want to be loved

30 nov 20

today
first day
of the rest of my life
brand new
a whole day
home alone
with nothing
and everything
to do
be
spontaneous
me

spiritual practice first
whenever possible
then play
and pray
overflowing gratitude
this one precious moment
is all there is

in eastern Indian
spiritual tradition
one of the practices
is devotional
ecstatic
chanting
kirtan
call and response

rock my soul
Sanskrit phrases
naming
gods and goddesses
the idea is if I
repeat the name of the goddess
with my heart open
the vibration of the sounds
eventually shakes
my soul into being Her
or Him
depending on the chant

naming limits infinity

1 dec 20

2 dec 20

was it a lost day
a day I didn't practice
didn't rite
that slipped out

write
rite
ritual
practice
ceremony
meditation
drumming
chanting
shaking
help
me
be
now
here
present

present too
when I level
kitchen cabinet doors
if joy and gratitude is present

so am I
I am

spirit
play of words
often so
synchronistic

how do I
show the immensity
of what I feel
when there's so much
danger out there
and I could get seriously hurt
if I live with a guarded heart
I'm not living
walking dead

most everyone

open heart
live so fully
I'm bursting
as if this day
is my last

fearless
trusting
in the face of danger
my end is already decided
so Krishna tells Arjuna
in the Bhagavad Gita

3 dec 20

I had a video conference
with my doc this morning
so much better than driving into town

osteopenia
I have it
pre osteoporosis
I've shrunk 3 inches
in 3 years
20% chance of a hip fracture
in the next 10 years

doc wants me to take drugs
yuck
not so keen on it

oh well
life goes on

if something's got to break
let my heart break wide open
so it can no longer close

let me stay wide open
to all of life's everything
feel deeply
each precious moment

growing up
in my family
if I opened my arms
to give a hug
I'd often get belly punched
with my brother saying
"you're wide open"

being wide open
breaks all the rules
being wide open
is dangerous
might get punched in the gut

being closed
is a slow dull death
no pain
no joy
just dull
boring
no adventure
no risk

fear and divisiveness
are such powerful motivators

trust is more powerful
break all the rules

how can I trust more

4 dec 20

so what's wrong with addiction
as I reach for my cuppa Joe
and sip
that delicious
aroma

savor the moment

when I don't drink coffee
in approximately 24 hours
I get a bad headache

is the pain worth it
for the pleasure of the moment

that first sensation
of bliss
tension leaving
highly energized

that's meditation

addiction is yearning
to connect with spirit
feeling blocked within
from finding
connection
with source
looking outside for the love

we weren't taught to give ourselves

it's there
hiding
nowhere to go
but in

starts with
unconditional compassion
unconditional forgiveness
no matter what was done
in the past
by whom

anger towards another
hurts me the most
when I cannot stand
how I feel inside
I distance from the feeling
addiction buffers
feeling is still there
gets bigger when
dishonored

cycle

stop the wheel
meditate
remember
connection
with spirit
where we come from

where we return

life is short

5 dec 20

hubris

I just realized I started writing
before candle and gong
sign of hubris
ego
I definitely have one

now the gong
breathe
7 minutes it took
for awareness
not being present
with my Muse
spirit

I'd been thinking
about work
in those 7 minutes

thinking about how
to shake the tree
without getting fired

troublemaker

always been one
I wonder why

blessed from birth
showered with unconditional love
from my Nana
Auschwitz survivor
who said
I was the first being
who brought love back into her life

love is infinite
not limited
not conditional
unconditional
the more I love myself
the more love I receive
what I give
I get
law of reciprocity
I just made that up

trusting me and spirit
are a team
spirit is boss
gives me
the inner strength
to speak up for
what I believe to
be right and just

gong gong gong

6 dec 20

dear friend's son
just tested positive
for covid
he's on the spectrum
for perceiving and
experiencing way differently
than most folk

energy for the best possible
outcome is spirit's hands
no matter what I do
so I choose to be
the best me
vessel of love
gratitude
freedom
peace
trust

maybe this is a wakeup call
for everyone
how to be more
aware
fearless
trusting inner strength
to heal whole holy

how to describe the changes
he's feeling in his body
so many questions spinning

7 dec 20

fire ceremony tonight
in times like these
when it's safer to be apart
because the government didn't
do its job protecting us from a pandemic
they knew was coming

whoever is responsible
for the spread of the
virus
doesn't matter

it's here
how do we now
take care
of ourselves
and each other
as responsibly
as we can

that was a rant
there's way more
but not now

I was going to say
at 7pm on the 7th
of each month
we light a fire
to help cleanse

waters of the world
gratitude Joseph Rael
beautiful painted arrow

let's be together in ceremony
in our separate homes
in our connected hearts

ha
lit the candle
forgot the gong

from not aware
to aware
changes
in a flash

choices
unconscious
then ding ding ding
wake up

before I set the timer
thoughts running
through my head
on how
given the choice
with limited time
I more often choose
to neglect body
stretching
preening

and forego
that part of my practice

like that's not as important
as the writing
and meditation parts

stretching
just breathing
very slowly
with care
mindful to support
and not move too quickly

when I come to an edge of
discomfort
tightness
if it hurts too much
back off
otherwise
stay there
breathe
if I can hold
the position
19 breaths
40 seconds minimum
more isn't necessary
muscles reorient
there's more ease
come back to center

bodies are miracles

science discovers that every day
what mystics have known
forever

we are miracles
let's treat each other
all living beings
with the respect
we deserve
simply because
we exist

why do some people
think they are better than others

because inside each of them
at times inside of me
there's a fight to the death
between one learned part and another

those parts create drama

8 dec 20

the bells are ringing
gongs
I remember today
background song lyrics
niggle to the surface
the bells are ringing
for me and my gal
Judy Garland and Gene Kelly
1942

will classics be remembered

entertainers
on the big screen
no more movie houses
theatres close
dance halls
clubs
no more
is it safe to gather

unsafe
in the pandemic

how being in
the outside world
is changing

in many ways
forcing us
to be inside
within
be with ourselves
not run away
distracted by outside drama

an incredible opportunity
to meditate
notice what comes up
without judgment
really go inside
exploring

who the heck am I
what am I doing here
what's really important

I can answer
those three questions
with one word

love

I could say
joy
peace
bliss
gratitude
passion
compassion

all different
facets of

love

about the author

Jo Levkoff is a poet, compassionate witness and deep listener. She is the author of Promoting Healthy Preschoolers and Families, a retired licensed professional counselor and approved supervisor through the American Association of Marriage and Family Therapy. She currently offers Heart and Soul Touch Guidance through video conferencing, phone, text, or email with individuals, couples, partners and groups who want to go deeper together. (www.alliesonthepath.com)

www.ingramcontent.com/pod-product-compliance
Lightning Source LLC
LaVergne TN
LVHW091027080826
845145LV00002B/383

* 9 7 8 0 5 7 8 8 6 8 4 8 6 *